READ THIS!

Fascinating Stories from the Content Areas

Intro

Daphne Mackey

With
Wendy Asplin
Laurie Blass
Deborah Gordon
Mary March

TEACHER'S MANUAL

CAMBRIDGE UNIVERSITY PRESS
Cambridge, New York, Melbourne, Madrid, Cape Town,
Singapore, São Paulo, Delhi, Mexico City

Cambridge University Press
32 Avenue of the Americas, New York, NY 10013-2473, USA

www.cambridge.org
Information on this title: www.cambridge.org/9781107649231

First published 2012
2nd printing 2013

Printed in the United States of America

A catalog record for this publication is available from the British Library.

ISBN 978-1-107-63071-0 Student's Book
ISBN 978-1-107-64923-1 Teacher's Manual

Layout services: Page Designs International, Inc.
Audio production: John Marshall Media

Contents

Introduction

Read This! is a four-level reading series for beginning, low intermediate, and intermediate-level English learners. The series is designed to enhance students' confidence and enjoyment of reading in English, build their reading skills, and develop their vocabulary.

The readings in the series are high interest and content-rich. They are all nonfiction and contain fascinating true information. The style of writing makes the information easily digestible, and the language is carefully controlled at each level to make the texts just challenging enough, but easily accessible.

Each book in *Read This!* consists of five thematically related units. Each unit is loosely connected to a different academic discipline that might be studied in an institution of higher education, such as business, engineering, psychology, health care, or mathematics. Each unit is divided into three chapters, and each chapter contains a reading accompanied by exercise material. Besides the main theme of the unit, each chapter is tied to a secondary academic content area, so that students can experience an interdisciplinary approach to a topic.

Accompanying each reading is a variety of pre- and postreading activities. They are designed to provide a balance of reading comprehension, vocabulary, and reading skill development. Many activities also provide opportunities for student discussion and a chance for students to connect the topics of the readings to their own lives and experience. Each unit ends with a wrap-up that reviews ideas and vocabulary from all three chapters of the unit.

Vocabulary instruction is an important focus of *Read This!* Selected words from each reading are previewed, presented, practiced, and recycled. These words are drawn from the two academic disciplines that are brought together in each reading. In addition, selected words from the Academic Word List (AWL) are pulled out from each reading for instruction.

Each unit is designed to take 6–9 hours of class time, depending on how much out-of-class work is assigned by the teacher. The units can either be taught in the order they appear or out of sequence. It is also possible to teach the chapters within a unit out of order. However, by teaching the units and chapters in sequence, students will benefit fully from the presentation, practice, and recycling of the target vocabulary.

All the readings in the *Read This!* series have been recorded for those students whose language learning can be enhanced by listening to a text as well as by reading it. However, since the goal of the series is to build students' readings skills, students should be told to read and study the texts without audio before they choose to listen to them.

The audio files can be found on the *Read This!* Web site at www.cambridge.org/readthis. Students can go to this site and listen to the audio recordings on their computers, or they can download the audio recordings onto their personal MP3 players to listen to them at any time.

An audio CD of the readings is also available in the back of this Teacher's Manual for those teachers who would like to bring the recorded readings into their classroom for students to hear.

The following section of this Teacher's Manual provides background information and general suggestions for teaching each section of the Student's Book. Following these general suggestions are specific suggestions for teaching activities in each chapter. In addition, answers to all activities are provided.

General Teaching Suggestions

Unit Opener

The title, at the top of the first page of each unit, names the academic content area that unifies the three chapters in the unit. The title of each chapter also appears, along with a picture and a short blurb that hints at the content of the chapter reading. These elements are meant to intrigue readers and whet their appetites for what is to come. At the bottom of the page, the main academic content area of the unit is repeated, and the secondary academic content area for each chapter is given as well.

1. Preview the main academic content area of the unit by encouraging students to consider what they know about the topic. For example, ask *What subject matter do students normally study in this academic content area? What sorts of jobs do people get after studying this content area?* Another option is to lead a class brainstorm. Have students call out the words and phrases they associate with the main academic content area, and list them on the board.
2. Look at the chapter titles and the blurb below the pictures. Check that students understand the meaning of the titles and the blurb. Don't spend too much time having students predict what the readings will be about since this is always a question that they will be asked at the end of the Topic Preview section of each chapter.
3. The unit-opening page also gives the secondary academic content area of each chapter. Students might be less familiar with some of these areas, such as cosmetology, information technology, physiology, culinary arts, or biomedical science. Again, see how much students know about these content areas and what sorts of jobs are possible for people who study in these fields.
4. Finally, ask students to think about how the two academic content areas might interconnect. For example, the main content area of Unit 3 in *Read This! 1* is mathematics. The secondary disciplines for the chapters are sociology, cosmetology, and music. Get students thinking about the possible connections between math and music, for example, or math and the study of beauty.

1 Topic Preview

The opening page of each chapter includes a picture and two tasks: Part A and Part B. Part A is usually a problem-solving task in which students are asked to bring some of their background knowledge or personal opinions to bear. Part B always consists of three discussion questions that draw students closer and closer to an idea of what the reading is about. In fact, the last question, *What do you think the reading will be about?* is always the same in every chapter: This is to help learners get into the habit of predicting what texts will be about before they read.

1. Have students describe the picture to a partner. Suggest appropriate *Wh-* questions for them to ask and answer in their discussion, and write them on the board. For example, *Who do you see in the picture? Where are these people? What are they doing? When does this take place?*
2. Move on to Part A. Since this task provides students with an opportunity to personalize the topic, it's a good idea to have them complete the task individually first. Then have students share their answers with a partner or the whole class.
3. Have students work in pairs or small groups to answer the discussion questions in Part B. Then have the groups share their answers with the class.

2 Vocabulary Preview

This section has students preview selected words that appear in the reading. It contains two tasks: Part A and Part B. Part A presents selected words for the students to study and learn. Part B has the students check their understanding of these words.

In Part A, the selected words are listed in three boxes. The box on the left contains words that relate to the main content area of the unit. The box on the right contains words that relate to the secondary content area of the reading. Between these two boxes are words from the reading that come from the Academic Word List (AWL). Placing the AWL words between the two lists of content area words creates a visual representation of the fact that the content area words are specific to separate content areas, while the AWL words are general academic words that might appear in either content area.

Note that the part of speech of a word is given in the chart only if this word could also be a different part of speech. Also note that some words are accompanied by words in parentheses. This alerts students to some common collocations that can form with the word and that will appear in the reading.

The vocabulary in the Vocabulary Preview is recycled over and over. The words appear in the reading; in

Section 5, Vocabulary Check; in the unit Wrap-Up; and in the unit test.

1. It's important that students understand the meaning of the selected key words from the reading. Have students study the words listed in Part A. Have them put a check next to the words that they are confident they know well. Instruct students to do this task individually and then compare answers with a partner. Students can then help each other if one knows a word that the other doesn't.
2. You can decide how you want to treat the words that neither student knows. You can either have students look up the meaning of those words in a dictionary or wait until the whole class comes back together and then go over the words. During pair work, circulate among the students, taking notes on any words that you may want to spend more time clarifying. Then bring those words up for the whole class to discuss.
3. In Part B, students check their understanding of the meaning of the selected words. Have students complete the task individually and then compare answers with a partner. Then elicit and write the answers on the board, so that students can check.

3 Reading

This section contains the reading and accompanying photos or illustrations. Some words from the reading are glossed at the bottom of the page. These are low-frequency words that students are not expected to know. Understanding these words might be important for understanding the reading; however, it would probably not be useful for students to incorporate the words into their active vocabulary.

The icon at the top of the Student Book's page indicates that the reading is available as an MP3 file online. Students can access this by going to the *Read This!* Web site at www.cambridge.org/readthis.

1. Before students read the text, have them look at the art and speculate about how it relates to the reading.
2. Next have students preview the questions in Reading Check Part A, which immediately follows the reading. Then have students read, emphasizing that they should try to read the text through quickly without stopping, in order to get the main ideas.
3. After the students' first reading of the text, elicit answers to the questions in Reading Check Part A. Review the answers with the class, and field any questions that may arise.
4. Have students read the text a second time.

4 Reading Check

This section is designed to check students' comprehension of the text. Part A checks their understanding of the main ideas. Part B asks students to retrieve more detailed information from the reading.

1. Students will have answered the questions in Part A immediately after their first reading of the text.
2. Have students answer the questions in Part B after they complete their second reading of the text. One option is for students to work in pairs or small groups. Then have a reporter from each pair or group write the answers on the board or call out the answers in class.
3. During the reporting activity, always ask students to justify their answers. Have them go back to the reading to show why they think their answers are correct. If the questions are multiple choice or true / false, have students explain why the other answer(s) cannot be correct.

5 Vocabulary Check

In this section, students revisit the same vocabulary that they studied before they read the text and that they have since encountered in the reading. The Vocabulary Check contains two tasks: Part A and Part B. In Part A, students are asked to complete a text by choosing appropriate vocabulary words for the context. The text in Part A is essentially a summary of the most salient information in the reading. This activity both reinforces the target vocabulary for the chapter and the content of the reading.

Part B varies from chapter to chapter. Sometimes it has a game-like quality, where students have to unscramble a word or find the odd word out in a group of words. Sometimes the task helps students extend their understanding of the target words by working with other parts of speech derived from the words. Other times, the task tests students' knowledge of other words that the target words often co-occur with (their collocations).

1. Have students work on Part A individually and then check their answers in pairs. Review answers with the whole class.
2. Explain the purpose of Part B before students begin. For example, you may need to explain what a collocation is, or you may want to review the relevant word forms. Have students work on Part B, either individually or in pairs. Then elicit answers and field questions.

6 Applying Reading Skills

An important strand of *Read This!* is reading skill development. Students are introduced to a variety of skills, such as finding main ideas and supporting details, identifying cause and effect, and organizing information from a reading into a chart. Practicing these skills will help students gain a deeper understanding of the content of the reading and the author's purpose. The section opens with a brief explanation of the reading skill and why it is important.

This section has two tasks: Part A and Part B. In Part A, students usually work with some kind of graphic organizer that helps them practice the skill and organize information. This work will prepare them to complete Part B.

1. Introduce the reading skill. Give examples of when this skill might be useful, such as preparing for a test or writing a report for class or at work. Then have students complete Part A. If necessary, model the first item to ensure that students understand the directions. Have students work individually and then review answers in pairs or as a class. Clarify as necessary.
2. Part B is similar to Part A, but usually more challenging. Have students complete this task either individually, in pairs, or in small groups. Review their work as a class and give feedback.

7 Discussion

This section contains three questions that will promote engaging discussion and encourage students to connect the ideas and information in the readings to their own knowledge and experience. Many of the questions take students beyond the readings. There is also ample opportunity for students to express their opinions. This activity can help students consolidate their understanding of the readings and practice new vocabulary.

1. Have students discuss the questions in pairs or small groups, taking turns to answer each question. Encourage students to develop their ideas by asking each other questions, such as *What do you mean?* or *Could you say more about that?*
2. Conclude the activity by inviting individuals to share their opinions and ideas with the class.

Wrap-Up

Each unit ends with a Wrap-Up, which gives students the chance to review vocabulary and ideas from the unit. It will also help them prepare for the unit test (see pages 33–51 of this Teacher's Manual). Teachers may want to pick and choose which parts of the Wrap-Up they decide to have students do, since to do all the activities for every unit might be overly time-consuming. The Wrap-Up section consists of the following:

Vocabulary Review

All the target vocabulary from the three chapters of the unit is presented in a chart. The chart is followed by an activity in which students match definitions to words in the chart.

Vocabulary in Use

Students engage in mini-discussions in which they use some of the target language from the unit. Students will be able to draw on their personal experience and knowledge of the world.

Interview

Students work with the concepts of the readings by participating in a structured and imaginative oral activity. The interviews require that the students have understood and digested the content of at least one of the readings in a chapter. One advantage of interviews is that they are self-leveling. In other words, the sophistication of the interview is determined by the level and oral proficiency of the students. Students will need help in preparing for the interviews. They will also need time to prepare for them. It might be a good idea for the teacher to model the first interview with one of the stronger students in the class.

Writing

This section of the Wrap-Up provides the teacher with an opportunity to have students do some writing about the content of the unit. The setup of this section varies from unit to unit.

WebQuest

For those students, programs, or classrooms that have Internet access, students can log onto www.cambridge.org/readthis. They can then find the WebQuest for the unit that they have been studying. The WebQuest is essentially an Internet scavenger hunt in which students retrieve information from Web sites that they are sent to. In this way, students encounter the information from the chapters once more. The Web sites confirm what they have already read and then broaden their knowledge of the unit topics by leading them to additional information. The WebQuests may be done individually or in pairs. Students may either submit their answers to the teacher online or they can print an answer sheet, complete it by hand, and hand it in to the teacher.

1 Education

For general suggestions on how to teach each section of a unit, see pages v–vii of this Teacher's Manual.

Unit Opener (page 1)

1. Activate students' background knowledge with a class brainstorm. With books closed, draw a circle and write *Education* in the center. Draw lines coming out of the circle. Ask students to list different education words and ideas, and write them on the lines. Prompt them with words like *teachers*, *students*, *books*, *classes*, *tests*, *school rules*, *elementary schools*, *high schools*, *colleges*, etc.
2. Ask students questions, such as *Which parts of school do you like?* and *Which parts of school do you not like?* Ask students to put up their hands if they like tests and exams. Ask them how tests and exams make them feel. Then ask students what time school begins in the morning. Have them put up their hands if they like getting up very early for school. You can also ask students to think about school rules. Ask them who creates or makes the rules in schools.
3. Have students open their books to page 1 and read the three chapter titles. Have them also look at the pictures and say what they see, working either in pairs or as a class. Read the short "teaser" blurbs with the class and answer any questions.
4. Write the following three content areas on the board: *Biology*, *Government*, *Psychology*. Elicit or explain as necessary what kinds of things are studied in each secondary content area. (*Biology is the study of the body. What are the names of some people in government? What are the names of the school officials in your school? A psychologist is a person who helps people with problems.*) Explain that each chapter will be about education, but it will also relate to one of the content areas on the board.

Chapter 1 Late Start

1 Topic Preview (page 2)

Part A

1. Have students briefly describe the picture to a partner and then share their ideas with the class. Ask questions, such as *What time do you think it is in the picture? Does the teen want to get up? What time do you get up for work or school in the morning? What time do you go to bed at night? Is it easy or hard to get up? How do you feel in the morning? Do you think clearly in the morning? How many hours of sleep do you get?*
2. Review the directions with the class, and make sure students understand all the sleep habits in the list. Clarify vocabulary as necessary. If some students are parents of children or teens, have them change the *My Parents* column title to *My Children.*
3. Listen to different answers and have a class discussion about sleep habits, comparing the habits of young people and older people.

Part B

1. Before students discuss the questions, have them reread the chapter title and look at the picture again.
2. Ask students to think about what an *ideal* wake-up time for them is and what an *ideal* amount of hours of sleep is. Then have them discuss the three questions. Make sure they discuss how the teen pictured probably feels and where the teen has to go.
3. When discussing their answers to question 3, point out that there aren't any right or wrong answers.

2 Vocabulary Preview (page 3)

Part B Answers

1. grade	6. drop out
2. absent	7. alert
3. administrator	8. body clock
4. tired	9. adult
5. illness	10. result

3 Reading (pages 4–5)

This reading is about schools changing their start times to better accommodate the optimum learning times for teens. It uses biology to explain the reason teens' learning times are better later in the morning, and compares adult and teen body clocks.

1. Introduce the reading with a class discussion about the pictures. Start with the picture on page 4 of the girl sleeping in class. Ask questions, such as *Where is this person? What time do you think it is? What is this person doing?* Then have students look at the

picture of the alert students on page 5. Ask additional questions, such as *How do the students look in the second picture? What is a possible reason? What do you think is the connection between the two pictures? What do you think is the connection between the pictures and the title of the reading?*

2. Before they start reading, have students preview the questions in Part A of the Reading Check on page 6. Check students' comprehension of the questions.

4 Reading Check (page 6)

Part A Answers

1. F	2. T	3. F

Part B Answers

1. a	3. b	5. a	7. a
2. c	4. a	6. c	8. c

5 Vocabulary Check (page 7)

Part A Answers

1. tired	6. grades
2. alert	7. illnesses
3. body clock	8. absent
4. adults	9. drop out
5. results	10. administrators

Part B Answers

1. a	4. an
2. an	5. A
3. An	

6 Applying Reading Skills (page 8)

Part A

1. Have the class look at the description of the reading skill. Explain that there is a reading skill in every chapter. Each reading skill task has two parts, A and B, and the parts are connected to each other.
2. Make sure students understand what *main idea* and *paragraph* mean.
3. Have students read the statements. Explain that they will not be able to find the exact sentence in each paragraph. If students already know about topic sentences, point out that the three statements listed are not topic statements, but rather statements summarizing the main idea of a paragraph.
4. Have students find the paragraphs in the reading that match each main idea. If necessary, do one as an example.
5. After they complete the exercise, tell students it is easier to understand the reading if they know the main idea of each paragraph.

Answers

1. Paragraph 3	3. Paragraph 6
2. Paragraph 1	

Part B

1. Point out to students that they will now be looking for the main ideas of the remaining paragraphs.
2. To check answers, have students compare their answers in pairs. Tell them to explain their answers if they are not the same as their partners' answers.

Answers

1. a	2. b	3. a

7 Discussion (page 8)

1. Start the discussion of question 1 by eliciting the differences between adult and teen body clocks. Then have students compare their typical sleep habits to adult and teen body clocks and identify which is more similar to theirs.
2. Have different pairs or groups tell the class their favorite times and their most alert times. Then have them discuss their activities at those times. You might want to divide the students into groups by their favored time of day and compare reasons as to why.
3. For question 3, students need to use what they have learned in the reading and apply it to the question. Explain that the answer is not in the reading. Ask students to brainstorm in their pairs or groups, a list of possible problems and then share their list with the class.

Chapter 2
First Write . . . It Helps!

1 Topic Preview (page 9)

Part A

1. Have students look at the picture. Elicit what the student who is standing is doing. Ask *Does the student look comfortable? Relaxed? Nervous? Does it look like this is an easy thing for him to do?* Have students discuss why reading or speaking in front of a group of people would make someone nervous. Also have them discuss how they would feel.
2. Make sure students understand the task and the activities listed.
3. After students complete the task, have students compare their answers in groups. You could also do a tally of the ratings on the board to see which of the activities were most often rated as the two most difficult.

Part B

1. For question 1, have students look back at their two choices from Part A and choose the one that is the most difficult. Have them give reasons for their choices.
2. For question 2, ask students to discuss how the student who is standing probably feels. You might also introduce the idea of consequences by asking students what the student is probably most nervous about: *Is he nervous about making a mistake? Is he worried about what the other students will think or what the teacher will think?*
3. Have students revisit the title and make predictions about the story they are about to read.

2 Vocabulary Preview (page 10)

Part B Answers

1. focus	6. file
2. brain	7. experiment
3. relax	8. study
4. information	9. stress
5. memory	10. score

3 Reading (pages 11–12)

This reading explains how writing can help reduce stress. It gives suggestions on how to use writing for this purpose and the different situations in which writing might be helpful.

1. Introduce the reading with a discussion about the pictures. Ask students what the students in the first picture are doing. Ask them if they think the test the students are taking is a small quiz or an important test and to give reasons for their thoughts. Then ask them how important tests, such as this one, normally make them feel. You might also want to ask students about any techniques or strategies they use to make themselves feel less nervous or stressed.
2. Before they start reading, have students preview the questions in Part A of the Reading Check on page 13.

4 Reading Check (page 13)

Part A Answers

1. b	2. c	3. a

Part B Answers

1. T	3. T	5. T	7. F
2. F	4. T	6. T	8. F

5 Vocabulary Check (page 14)

Part A Answers

1. study	6. memory
2. stress	7. files
3. focus	8. relaxes
4. information	9. experiments
5. brains	10. scores

Part B Answers

1. verb	4. verb
2. noun	5. verb
3. noun	6. noun

6 Applying Reading Skills (page 15)

1. Look at the description of the reading skill with the students and review the relationship between cause and effect. You may want to do this by putting on the board a simple cause and effect relationship such as *walking in the rain* (*cause*) and *getting wet* (*effect*), or *doing your homework* (*cause*) and *getting an A on the test* (*effect*). Ask students to draw an arrow between the two phrases to show the cause and effect relationship.
2. Point out that it is helpful to notice when a reading has cause and effect relationships because differentiating the cause from the effect will help increase comprehension of the reading.
3. Have students complete the tasks. Then review answers with the class to make sure students have understood the cause and effect relationship.

Part A Answers

1. b	2. a	3. c

Part B Answers

1. b	2. a	3. a

7 Discussion (page 15)

1. For question 1, prime the discussion by asking *What are the different ways your body feels when you are nervous?*
2. For questions 2 and 3, encourage students to give specific examples.

Chapter 3 Student Government

1 Topic Preview (page 16)

Part A

1. Check students' understanding of the word *decisions*. You may want to contrast it with *choices* to help them understand.
2. After students have completed their answers, go over their answers as a class.

Part B

1. For question 1, have students think about the types of things they make decisions about in English class.
2. For question 2, have students look at the picture and describe the situation. Ask them where they think these students are and what they might be talking about. Also ask them to notice the ages of the students and the number of adults in the room.
3. Have students revisit the title and make predictions about the story they are about to read.

2 Vocabulary Preview (page 17)

Part B Answers

1. vote	6. curriculum
2. graduate	7. leader
3. budget	8. administration
4. interact	9. govern
5. rule	10. democratic

3 Reading (pages 18–19)

This reading is about a school that believes in giving its students control over the rules and regulations of all aspects of running the school. It explains both the process and the result of this unique approach.

1. Introduce the reading with a class discussion about the pictures. Ask students to say where they think these people are and what they might be doing. Explain that the students are in a meeting about the administration of a school. Ask *What do you think these people are talking about? What decisions do school administrators need to make?*
2. Before they start reading, have students preview the questions in part A of the Reading Check on page 20.

4 Reading Check (page 20)

Part A Answers

1. c	2. a	3. a

Part B Answers

1. F	3. T	5. T	7. T
2. F	4. F	6. F	8. T

5 Vocabulary Check (page 21)

Part A Answers

1. democratic
2. vote
3. govern
4. administration
5. leaders
6. curriculum
7. budget
8. rule
9. interact
10. graduates

Part B Answers

1. about
2. on
3. on
4. of
5. with

Answers

SUDBURY VALLEY SCHOOL STUDENTS

help govern their school
make important school decisions
often interact with people of all ages
decide on punishment
vote on the budget

STUDENTS IN MOST SCHOOLS

do not help govern their school
don't make important school decisions
don't often interact with people of all ages
don't decide on punishment
don't vote on the budget

6 Applying Reading Skills (page 22)

Part A

1. Look at the description of the reading skill with students and review the concept of note taking.
2. Explain that some readings will have a lot of comparisons in them, and that it can be helpful to list the comparisons in a chart to make the reading easier to understand.

Answers

1. T
2. F
3. T
4. T
5. F

Part B

1. Check that students understand the structure of the chart and the types of information that should go in the different columns. You may also want to review the structure of negative statements with your students.
2. Have students compare their charts in pairs or groups.

7 Discussion (page 22)

1. For question 1, have students talk about the daily decisions they make about school and your class. You may want to have them categorize small and big decisions (e.g., what kind of paper or writing tool to use, when to do homework).
2. Ask them to list the different types of decisions that they make. Point out that when they work in groups or pairs, they often need to make decisions with other people. Ask them to compare the processes of making decisions alone and making decisions with others. Ask them which one is easier and which is harder, and to say why.
3. After having students discuss which decisions are made for them by other people, you may want to ask if there are some decisions they think they should make for themselves instead, and if so, why.

Unit 1 Wrap-Up

Vocabulary Review (page 23)

Answers

1. tired
2. administrator
3. drop out
4. absent
5. focus
6. study
7. score
8. experiment
9. interact
10. budget
11. rule
12. govern

Vocabulary in Use (page 24)

Answers will vary

Interview (page 24)

1. Introduce the activity by asking the class to think about all three stories. Have students review the titles and the pictures for each of the three chapters.
2. Explain that the students are going to ask each other the questions. Check that they understand the questions. Then put them into pairs. Have students take turns asking and answering the questions. Tell them to listen for differences in their answers and to discuss those differences.

Writing (page 24)

1. Instruct students to look for mistakes in the paragraph.
2. Have them copy the paragraph and give it a title (something different from the title of the chapter).

Possible Answer

Democratic Schools

A democratic school is opening soon. These schools are not a new idea. They are not similar to / not like most other schools. At democratic schools, the students govern. Students make all the decisions at meetings once a week. At these meetings, students vote on everything. Democratic school students learn to be leaders.

WebQuest (page 24)

At the time of publication, the links in the WebQuests were accurate and the content was deemed to be appropriate. However, Web sites change over time. It is therefore recommended that you go to the Web sites before assigning the WebQuests to make sure that the links are still current and the content is relevant and appropriate for your students. We continually monitor the Web sites and will make changes to the questions if the Web sites change or disappear. In such cases, you will have to work out the answers to those questions yourself.

Answers

1. A student is sleeping on his books.
2. between 11 a.m. and 1 p.m.
3. 19
4. Sian Beilock / a psychology professor (at the University of Chicago in Illinois)
5. to stop (something) from happening or existing
6. math
7. weekly
8. one
9. one
10. Answers will vary.

2 Sociology

For general suggestions on how to teach each section of a unit, see pages v–vii of this Teacher's Manual.

Unit Opener (page 25)

1. With books closed, write *Sociology* on the board. Activate students' background knowledge with a class brainstorm. Ask *How many words about sociology do you know?* Prompt them with words like *culture*, *marriage*, *teenagers*, *Facebook* (or other social networking Web sites). Write these words on the board.
2. Ask students questions, such as *What are some ways to divide people into groups?* (*by culture*, *income level*, *interests*, *politics*, *religion*) Personalize the discussion by asking *What groups are you part of?* List some of the groups on the board (*family*, *gender*, *age*, *school*, *sports*, *neighborhood*, *style of dress*).
3. Have students look at the content areas at the bottom of the page. Explain that each chapter will be about sociology, but it will also relate to one of these content areas: architecture, anthropology, or literature. Elicit, or explain as necessary, what kinds of things are studied in each of the secondary content areas. (*An architect is a person who designs buildings. What is your favorite building? What do you like about its architecture? Sociology and anthropology are similar. Sociology is the study of society – how people behave in groups or alone. Anthropology is the study of a culture from the past to the present. Literature refers to books, short stories, and poems. Why do people like to read? What is your favorite work of literature?*) Ask which "sociology" words on the board could also fit into each of the secondary content areas (culture *can be about anthropology*, neighborhood *can be about architecture*, interests *can be about literature*).
4. Have students look at the pictures and the titles of the three chapters. Read through the short "teaser" blurbs with the class and answer any questions.

Chapter 4
A Strange Place to Live!

1 Topic Preview (page 26)

Part A

1. Have students briefly describe the pictures to a partner and then share their ideas with the class. Ask questions, such as *Do you live in an apartment? Does this look like your living room? How is it the same? How is it different?*
2. Review the directions with the class. Clarify vocabulary as necessary.
3. Listen to different answers and have a class discussion about why different things might pose problems for older people.

Part B

1. Before students discuss the questions, have them read the chapter title and look at the pictures again. Ask students what they think *strange* means in this reading (*odd*, *unusual*; not *foreign*, *unknown*).
2. Questions 1 and 2 should elicit different types of living environments for seniors (*retirement homes*, *living with grown children*, *living alone*, etc.) and make students think about how life changes as people reach old age.

2 Vocabulary Preview (page 27)

Part B Answers

1. senior
2. apartment
3. shape
4. population
5. odd
6. design
7. ceiling
8. balcony
9. Elderly
10. independent

3 Reading (pages 28–29)

This reading is about apartments in Japan that are designed for seniors. It introduces the architects, Arakawa (Japanese, died in 2010) and Gins (American), who believe(d) that if our homes pose a daily challenge to us, both physically and mentally, we will live longer.

1. Introduce the reading with a class discussion about the pictures. Start with the picture on page 28. Ask questions, such as *Where was this picture taken? What do you see? What is strange about this apartment?* Then have students look at the picture of the person inside the apartment building on page 29. Ask additional questions, such as *Would you like to live in this apartment? Why or why not?*
2. Before they start reading, have students preview the questions in Part A of the Reading Check on page 30.

4 Reading Check (page 30)

Part A Answers

1. T	2. T	3. F

Part B Answers

1. b	3. a	5. b	7. b
2. a	4. b	6. c	

5 Vocabulary Check (page 31)

Part A Answers

1. apartment	5. elderly
2. odd	6. design
3. shapes	7. population
4. balcony	8. independent

Part B Answers

1. design	4. population
2. balcony	5. independent
3. senior	6. ceiling

6 Applying Reading Skills (page 32)

Part A

1. Have the class look at the description of the reading skill. Make sure students understand the meaning of *organizing* and *chart.*
2. Have students work individually to complete the task. Make it clear that they can put a check next to more than one item. Then have students compare their answers with a partner.
3. Go over the answers as a class.

Answers

✓ They have rooms with very bright colors.
✓ They have windows near the floor.
✓ They have very small doors.

Part B

1. Have students work individually to fill in the chart. Then have them compare their answers with a partner.
2. To check answers as a class, have students complete the chart on the board.

Answers

REGULAR APARTMENTS

have flat floors
have windows in the middle of the wall
are easy to walk in
have balconies with regular doors
any one of the following: have closets / are comfortable / don't always have very bright colors

ARAKAWA AND GINS' APARTMENTS

have very bright colors
have windows near the floor
have very small doors
any one of the following: are not comfortable / are not easy to walk around in / don't have flat floors / don't have windows in the middle of the wall / don't have regular doors to the balconies / don't have closets

7 Discussion (page 32)

1. Start the discussion of question 1 by asking if any students have elderly relatives. Ask *Where do they live? Do you think they would want to live in an Arakawa and Gins' apartment? Why or why not?*
2. For question 2, have students discuss their ideas in small groups. One person in the group should make two columns, writing the "good things" in one and the "bad things" in the other. Then have volunteers report to the class on their group's ideas. Poll the class. Say *Imagine you are an elderly person.* Then ask *Who wants to live in these apartments? Why or why not?*
3. For question 3, have students work in pairs before they share their answers with the whole class.

Chapter 5
King Peggy

1 Topic Preview (page 33)

Part A

1. Have students briefly describe the picture to a partner and then share their ideas with the class. Ask questions, such as *Do you think this person is important? Why?*
2. Clarify the meaning of *monarchy* if necessary. Make sure students understand the task.
3. After students complete the task, have a class discussion about monarchies. Ask questions, such as *Which countries have monarchies? Do you know the names of any of the kings or queens in those countries? Do you know the names of any princes or princesses? Emperors or empresses?* If possible, go online and find a map that shows which countries have monarchies, and share that with the class.

Answers

✓ Saudi Arabia has a monarchy.
✓ Some monarchies only have a king, never a queen.
✓ There are monarchies in Asia.

Part B

1. Before students discuss the questions, have them read the chapter title and look at the picture again.
2. For question 1, ask students to name any historical or contemporary women leaders they have heard of or know about.
3. For question 2, have students share their ideas in small groups and then as a class. Encourage students to give reasons for their opinions.
4. Have students revisit the title and make predictions about the story they are about to read.

2 Vocabulary Preview (page 34)

Part B Answers

1. Traditionally	6. female
2. assist	7. in charge
3. respect	8. royalty
4. tribe	9. elder
5. relative	10. ritual

3 Reading (pages 35–36)

This reading is about Peggy Bartels, an American who works in an office of the Ghana Embassy in Washington, D.C. After her uncle died in a small village in Ghana (in West Africa), she became the king.

1. Introduce the reading with a class discussion about the picture on page 35. Ask *Where do you think this is? Do you think she is the boss? Do you think she works for a boss?* Look at the map on page 36 and point out the location of Ghana.
2. Before they start reading, have students preview the questions in part A of the Reading Check on page 37.

4 Reading Check (page 37)

Part A Answers

1. b 2. c 3. a

Part B Answers

1. a	3. a	5. c	7. b
2. c	4. b	6. a	

5 Vocabulary Check (page 38)

Part A Answers

1. relative	6. female
2. tribe	7. assists
3. elders	8. royalty
4. traditionally	9. in charge
5. ritual	10. respect

Part B Answers

1. queen	4. never
2. king	5. respect
3. female	

6 Applying Reading Skills (page 39)

Part A

1. Have the class look at the description of the reading skill. Make sure students understand the concept of *order of events*. Point out that the reading on pages 35–36 is *not* in chronological order (it starts with the phone call to Peggy, but that event did not happen first in time). Students must think about what actually happened first, second, third, etc. – not the order of events in the reading.

2. Write a numbered list on the board (1–5), similar to the list on page 39 in the Student's Book. Next to number 1, write *The king of Otuam dies*.
3. Start to fill in the list of events with the help of the class. Tell students to look at the bulleted list and choose the next thing that happens in Peggy's story (*The elders choose Peggy as their new king.*). Write that on the second line in the list. Have students work with a partner to complete the list.

Answers

1. The king of Otuam dies.
2. The elders choose Peggy as their new king.
3. Peggy gets a phone call at 4:00 a.m.
4. The caller tells Peggy she is the new king.
5. Peggy accepts the job of king.

Part B

1. Have students work individually to number the steps in the correct order.
2. Check answers as a class by having volunteers write the steps in order on the board.

Answers

1 (c) The elders meet to choose a new king
2 (b) The elders say the names of all the king's relatives.
3 (e) The elders say Peggy's name and see a sign.
4 (a) The elders say Peggy's name two more times.
5 (d) The elders choose Peggy as the new king.

7 Discussion (page 39)

1. For question 1, start the discussion by asking *How do people in your country choose their leader?*
2. For questions 2 and 3, have students work in pairs and then share their ideas with the class.

Chapter 6 Quidditch: The World of Harry Potter Comes to Life

1 Topic Preview (page 40)

Part A

1. Review the directions with the class and make sure students understand that they should circle the answers that are true for them.
2. After students have chosen their answers, call on individuals to stand up and read one or more of their sentences aloud.
3. One sentence at a time, take a poll of the whole class. How many chose the first possibility? How many chose the second possibility? Discuss general opinions about sports that result from the poll.

Part B

1. Before students discuss the questions, have them look at the chapter title and the picture.
2. Have them discuss questions 1 and 2 in small groups. Then ask them to share answers as a class.
3. If needed, spend a little time discussing the Harry Potter series as a class. Explain, or ask one or more students to explain, the game of quidditch as played in the stories. Ask follow-up questions, such as *Does quidditch remind you of any other sport? Which one? Why?*

2 Vocabulary Preview (page 41)

Part B Answers

1. event	6. media
2. compete	7. reality
3. character	8. novel
4. in common	9. fiction
5. movement	10. reaction

3 Reading (pages 42–43)

This reading reports on how the game of quidditch, from the Harry Potter books, has become a fun, competitive sport at American colleges and universities.

1. Introduce the reading with a class discussion about the pictures. Ask questions, such as *Where do you think the people are playing? What sport do you think they are playing? What do you see in the second picture? What do you think is the connection between the two pictures?*
2. Before they start reading, have students preview the questions in part A of the Reading Check on page 44.

4 Reading Check (page 44)

Part A Answers

1. b 2. c 3. b

Part B Answers

1. F	4. T	7. F	10. T
2. F	5. F	8. T	
3. T	6. F	9. F	

5 Vocabulary Check (page 45)

Part A Answers

1. event
2. media
3. novels
4. character
5. in common
6. reality
7. movement

Part B Answers

1. a. competitive (*adj.*)
b. competition (*n.*)
c. compete (*v.*)
2. a. fiction (*n.*)
b. fictional (*adj.*)
3. a. react (*v.*)
b. reaction (*n.*)

6 Applying Reading Skills (page 46)

Part A

1. Have the class look at the description of the reading skill. Review what *scanning* means (*reading quickly to find particular information*). Emphasize that students should not read every word when they scan. Their eyes should stop only when they see the type of information they are looking for. Explain that scanning is especially useful when students are preparing for a test or doing research for an assignment.
2. Review the directions with the class and clarify the task. First, students only need to check the boxes that characterize the information in the left-hand column. If necessary, do the first item with the class as an example.
3. Have students go back to the reading to find and underline the specific names, numbers, and dates in the chart. Remind them to scan for the type of information they need. Ask questions, such as *What should you look for to find a date?* (*numbers*) *What should you look for to find a name?* (*capital letters*)

Answers

New York City: Name of a place
46: A number
2005: A date
Harry Potter: Name of a person
700: A number
Middlebury College: Name of a place

Part B

1. For the task, have students practice scanning the reading "Quidditch: The World of Harry Potter Comes to Life" on pages 42–43. Remind students that they need to read quickly in order to find the specific information in the list. When they finish, have them compare answers as a class.
2. As a follow-up, ask *What are some other things that scanning can help you do better?* (*find information on the Internet, look up a phone number, find something on a menu, read things that have a lot of details*, etc.)

Answers

1. Harry Potter
2. 2005
3. 46
4. New York City
5. Middlebury College
6. 700

7 Discussion (page 46)

1. To get the discussion going for question 1, ask *Why is quidditch so popular with college students?* Encourage students to give reasons with specific examples to support their answers.
2. For question 2, have students in small groups share their opinions about quidditch.
3. For question 3, have students in small groups share their answers to the questions. Then have them share their answers as a class.

Unit 2
Wrap-Up

Vocabulary Review (page 47)

Answers

1. odd
2. ceiling
3. design
4. independent
5. royalty
6. assist
7. relative
8. tribe
9. reaction
10. compete
11. media
12. novel

Vocabulary in Use (page 48)

Answers will vary

Interview (page 48)

1. Introduce the activity by asking the class to think about all three stories. Have students review the titles and the pictures for each of the three chapters.

2. Explain that the students are going to ask each other the questions. Check that they understand the questions. Then put them into pairs. Have students take turns asking and answering the questions. Tell them to listen for differences in their answers and to discuss those differences.

Writing (page 48)

Answer

A group of college students in Vermont wants to have some fun. They all love Harry Potter. The students decide to play quidditch. They make up rules and a scoring system. More and more students want to play. Today there are more than 500 quidditch teams around the world!

WebQuest (page 48)

At the time of publication, the links in the WebQuests were accurate and the content was deemed to be appropriate. However, Web sites change over time. It is therefore recommended that you go to the Web sites before assigning the WebQuests to make sure that the links are still current and the content is relevant and appropriate for your students. We continually monitor the Web sites and will make changes to the questions if the Web sites change or disappear. In such cases, you will have to work out the answers to those questions yourself.

Answers

1. Madeline Gins and Arakawa
2. East Hampton, New York / N.Y.
3. three / green, yellow, and purple
4. Eleanor Herman
5. happy
6. 7,000
7. Brooms Up: The Movie
8. Dewitt Clinton Park
9. quaffle

3 Science

For general suggestions on how to teach each section of a unit, see pages v–vii of this Teacher's Manual.

Unit Opener (page 49)

1. With books closed, write *Science* on the board. Activate students' background knowledge with a class brainstorm. Ask students *How many kinds of science are there?* Prompt them with words like *space* and *earth*. Write these words on the board.
2. Ask students questions, such as *Which kind of science is most interesting to you?* Broaden the discussion by asking *What is the name of a famous scientist?*
3. Have students look at the content areas at the bottom of the page. Explain that each chapter will be about science, but it will also relate to one of these content areas: engineering, medicine, and education. Elicit, or explain as necessary, what kinds of things are studied in each secondary content area. (*An engineer is a person who works in engineering. What do engineers make? What are the names of some jobs in medicine? Science education is important, but science classes are sometimes difficult. Is science easy or difficult for you? Why?*) Have students look at the pictures and the titles of the three chapters. Read through the short "teaser" blurbs with the class and answer any questions.

Chapter 7 Rescue in Chile

1 Topic Preview (page 50)

Part A

1. Have students briefly describe the picture to a partner and then share their ideas with the class. Ask questions, such as *What are the people doing? Why is it dangerous?*
2. Review the directions with the class and clarify vocabulary as necessary. Have students rank the jobs and then share their answers with the class.

Part B

1. Before students discuss the questions, have them read the chapter title and look at the picture again.
2. Have students discuss question 1. Listen to the different answers about things that come from mines such as gold, silver, coal, iron, and diamonds.

2 Vocabulary Preview (page 51)

Part B Answers

1. drill	6. mineral
2. surface	7. device
3. shaft	8. oxygen
4. dig	9. diagram
5. survive	10. finally

3 Reading (pages 52–53)

This reading is about a rescue of 33 miners trapped in a mine in Chile. It starts with the scene when the miners hear the drill. Then it goes back to tell the story from the beginning. It ends with the successful rescue.

1. Introduce the reading with a class discussion about the mine diagram. Ask questions, such as *What is the diagram of? Where is the old shaft? Where is the rescue shaft? Where are the miners?*
2. Before they start reading, have students preview the questions in Part A of the Reading Check on page 54.

4 Reading Check (page 54)

Part A Answers

1. b	2. c	3. a

Part B Answers

1. T	4. T	7. F	10. T
2. F	5. T	8. F	
3. T	6. F	9. F	

5 Vocabulary Check (page 55)

Part A Answers	
1. minerals	6. finally
2. dig	7. devices
3. oxygen	8. shaft
4. drill	9. surface
5. diagram	10. survive

Part B Answers	
1. noun	4. noun
2. verb	5. verb
3. verb	6. noun

6 Applying Reading Skills (page 56)

Part A

1. Have the class look at the description of the reading skill. *Scanning* means reading quickly to find particular information. Emphasize that students should not read every word when they scan. Their eyes should stop only when they find the information they are looking for. Explain that scanning is especially useful when students are preparing for a test or doing research for an assignment.
2. Review the directions with the class and clarify the task. Students simply need to check the boxes that characterize the information in the left-hand column. If necessary, do the first item with the class as an example.

Answers

2,220: A number
670: A number
August 5, 2010: A date
Chile: A name
Thirty-three: A number
540: A number
50: A number

Part B

1. For this task, have students practice scanning the reading on pages 52–53. Remind students that they need to read quickly to find the specific information in the list. When they finish, have them compare answers in pairs.
2. As a follow-up, ask *When can you use scanning?* (*to find information on the Internet, to look at a menu, to find a price or a location in an announcement*, etc.)

Answers	
1. 33	4. October 12
2. Chile	5. 68
3. 21 inches (53 centimeters)	

7 Discussion (page 56)

1. Start the discussion of question 1 by writing some adjectives on the board (e.g., *happy*, *worried*, *afraid*, etc.). Have students complete sentences about different stages of the experience: *At the beginning, they . . . On day 17, they . . .* This would be a good time to teach the past tense.
2. Regarding question 2, most mine rescues are not successful. The rescue in Chile was successful for three main reasons: (1) the miners found a shelter, (2) they worked together to share the food in the shelter, and (3) the rescue team on the surface did not give up. Many other countries also helped with knowledge and technology.
3. Regarding question 3, students will probably say money or high pay. In the case of miners, many live in areas far away from cities, and there are few other jobs available.

Chapter 8 Sleeping Beauty

1 Topic Preview (page 57)

Part A

1. Have students look at the picture and ask questions about it: *How does she feel?* (*tired, sleepy, unhappy*) *Do you feel this way? What time do you wake up? Do you always hear the alarm clock?*
2. Make sure students understand the task.
3. After students share their answers, find out the average number of hours that students in the class sleep.

Part B

1. For question 1, students will probably use the words *tired* and *sleepy*. You may also introduce the words *sad* and *depressed*.
2. For question 2, find out if students think the person in the picture is older or younger than they are.
3. Have students revisit the title and make predictions about the story they are about to read.

2 Vocabulary Preview (page 58)

Part B Answers

1. period	6. temperature
2. condition	7. symptom
3. normal	8. cure
4. affect	9. diagnose
5. rare	10. virus

3 Reading (pages 59–60)

This reading is about a girl named Louisa Ball, who has a rare condition that makes her sleep for long periods of time.

1. Introduce the reading with a class discussion about the pictures. Ask *Who is the person in the first picture? Do you know any stories about her? Who is the person in the second picture? What do you think is the connection between the title and the two pictures?*
2. Before they start reading, have students preview the questions in Part A of the Reading Check on page 61.

4 Reading Check (page 61)

Part A Answers

1. T 2. F 3. F

Part B Answers

1. b	3. a	5. c	7. b
2. c	4. a	6. b	8. b

5 Vocabulary Check (page 62)

Part A Answers

1. temperature	6. cure
2. diagnoses	7. rare
3. condition	8. affects
4. periods	9. symptoms
5. virus	10. normal

Part B Answers

1. cure	4. condition
2. rare	5. normal
3. period	6. diagnose

6 Applying Reading Skills (page 63)

Part A

1. Look at the description of the reading skill with students and review the concepts of *main ideas* and *supporting details*.
2. Point out that understanding how to identify main ideas and details is one of the most important ways to improve reading comprehension.
3. Have students work individually to complete the task. Then review answers with the class to make sure students have understood how to differentiate main ideas from details.

Answers

Main idea 1: Supporting details are *b* and *d*.
Main idea 2: Supporting details are *a* and *c*.

Part B

Possible Answers

any two of the following: KLS does not last forever. / It usually affects people for 8 to 12 years. / Louisa will probably have a normal life again someday.

7 Discussion (page 63)

1. For questions 1 and 2, ask students to list difficulties for people with KLS. Then have them number them in order of difficulty.
2. For question 2, encourage students to give specific examples.
3. For question 3, ask students if it's possible for people with KLS to finish high school, go to college, and have a job.

Chapter 9 Memory Palace

1 Topic Preview (page 64)

Part A

1. You may want to bring a deck of cards to class for this lesson.
2. Ask students *Do you like to play cards? Do you think you can remember the order of the cards?* Review the directions with the class.
3. After students have checked their answers, go over their answers in class.

Part B

1. After students discuss questions 1 and 2, if you brought cards, you could see how many students can really remember by showing 10 cards one by one, etc.
2. For question 2, have students describe the activity in the picture.
3. For question 3, have students make predictions about the story they are about to read.

2 Vocabulary Preview (page 65)

Part B Answers

1. researcher	6. human
2. memorize	7. practice
3. correctly	8. recall
4. ability	9. visual
5. mind	10. mental

3 Reading (pages 66–67)

This reading begins with a scene at a memory championship. It describes a technique for memorizing that many memory champions use.

1. Introduce the reading with a class discussion about the pictures. Ask students *How old are the people in the pictures? Where are they? What are they doing?*
2. Before they start reading, have students preview the questions in Part A of the Reading Check on page 68.

4 Reading Check (page 68)

Part A Answers

1. b	2. b	3. c

Part B Answers

1. F	4. F	7. T	10. F
2. T	5. T	8. T	
3. T	6. F	9. F	

5 Vocabulary Check (page 69)

Part A Answers

1. memorize	6. minds
2. recall	7. mental
3. correctly	8. humans
4. researchers	9. ability
5. visual	10. practice

Part B Answers

1. b	2. a	3. b	4. a

6 Applying Reading Skills (page 70)

Part A

1. Have the class look at the description of the reading skill. Make sure students understand what *order of events* means.

2. Draw a numbered list on the board. Read the list of events in Part A and make sure students understand them. Then ask *What happened first?* Elicit and write *The people sit at tables* next to number 1 on the board. Then ask students *What happened after that?* and so on. Make sure they find the answers in the list on page 70.
3. Have students complete the list in the book with a partner.

Part A Answers

1. The people sit at tables.
2. They pick up a deck of cards.
3. They memorize the order of the cards.
4. They put down the cards.
5. They get a second deck of cards.
6. They put the second deck in the same order as the first deck.
7. Someone checks the order of the second deck.

Part B

1. Have students work individually to number the steps in the correct order.
2. Check answers as a class by having volunteers write the steps in order on the board.

Part B Answers

1 (d) Choose a place for your memory palace.
2 (e) Imagine the inside of your memory palace.
3 (c) Imagine actions for each thing in your memory palace.
4 (b) Practice one time. Imagine a walk through the memory palace.
5 (a) Walk through your memory palace again later. You will recall everything.

7 Discussion (page 70)

1. For question 1, have students think of tasks that require a lot of memorization.
2. Regarding question 2, some people have tricks to help them memorize. For example, they make a word with the first letter of everything they need to remember.
3. Have students think of a few jobs and explain why a good memory is important for these jobs.

Unit 3 Wrap-Up

Vocabulary Review (page 71)

Answers

1. finally
2. drill
3. dig
4. surface
5. temperature
6. diagnose
7. rare
8. condition
9. correctly
10. human
11. researcher
12. memorize

Vocabulary in Use (page 72)

Answers will vary

Interview (page 72)

1. Introduce the activity by asking the class to think about all three stories. Have students review the titles and the pictures for each of the three chapters.
2. Explain that the students are going to ask each other the questions. Check that they understand the questions. Then put them into pairs. Have students take turns asking and answering the questions. Tell them to listen for differences in their answers and to discuss those differences.

Writing (page 72)

1. Instruct students to look for mistakes in the paragraph.
2. Have them copy the paragraph and give it a title (something different from the title of the chapter).

Possible Answer

Help for the Miners

After 17 days, there is good news from the mine in Chile. The 33 miners are alive! They are in a small place in the mine. It is 2,200 feet below the ground. Engineers on the surface are working on the rescue. A small rescue pod will go down the shaft.

WebQuest (page 72)

At the time of publication, the links in the WebQuests were accurate and the content was deemed to be appropriate. However, Web sites change over time. It is therefore recommended that you go to the Web sites before assigning the WebQuests to make sure that the links are still current and the content is relevant and appropriate for your students. We continually monitor the Web sites and will make changes to the questions if the Web sites change or disappear. In such cases, you will have to work out the answers to those questions yourself.

Answers

1. 24 in / 60 cm
2. a flag / a Chilean flag / the flag of Chile
3. Carlos Mamani Solis, 23
4. the United States (She is American.)
5. ten
6. 200 days or more
7. two times / twice
8. 2660 memorised
9. 30
10. Answers will vary.

4 Marketing

For general suggestions on how to teach each section of a unit, see pages v–vii of this Teacher's Manual.

Unit Opener (page 73)

1. With books closed, write *Marketing* on the board. Activate students' background knowledge with a class brainstorm. Ask them what the word *marketing* makes them think of (*store*, *buying*, *selling*, etc.), and write their ideas on the board.
2. Ask students questions, such as *What are some different ways to sell things? What do marketers do? Are you interested in studying marketing? Why or why not? Do you want to work in marketing? Why or why not?*
3. Have students look at the content areas at the bottom of the page. Explain that each chapter will be about marketing, but it will also relate to one of these content areas: computer studies, art and design, and travel and tourism. Elicit, or explain as necessary, what kinds of things are studied in each secondary content area.
4. Have students look at the pictures and the titles of the three chapters. Read through the short "teaser" blurbs with the class and answer any questions.

Chapter 10 FarmVille

1 Topic Preview (page 74)

Part A

1. Review the directions with the class, and make sure that students understand all the ways to learn about things to buy in the list. Clarify vocabulary as necessary. For item 5, explain that students need to come up with their own ideas on learning about things to buy.
2. Listen to different answers and have a class discussion about the best way to learn about things to buy.

Part B

1. Before students discuss the questions, have them read the chapter title and look at the picture. Ask students what they think *FarmVille* is.
2. Questions 1 and 2 should elicit that this is a picture from an online game. Ask students if the game is selling something – either in the game itself or in real life.

2 Vocabulary Preview (page 75)

Part B Answers

1. online	6. customer
2. click on	7. sales
3. goal	8. advertise
4. product	9. Awareness
5. brand	10. target

3 Reading (pages 76–77)

This reading is about an online game, FarmVille, that features product placement advertising for a particular company, Cascadian Farms. Cascadian Farms sells organic products. The passage also illustrates additional examples of product placement, such as in movies.

1. Introduce the reading with a class discussion about the pictures. Start with the picture on page 76. Ask questions, such as *What is the girl doing?* (*playing a computer game*) Then ask students to look at the picture on page 77. Ask questions, such as *Where are the people?* (*supermarket*) *What is the woman buying?* (*strawberries/fruit*) *What do you think is the connection between the pictures and the title of the reading?*
2. Before they start reading, have students preview the questions in Part A of the Reading Check on page 78.

4 Reading Check (page 78)

Part A Answers

1. c	2. b	3. a

Part B Answers

1. c	3. b	5. a	7. a
2. a	4. a	6. c	

5 Vocabulary Check (page 79)

Part A Answers	
1. advertise	5. click on
2. brand	6. awareness
3. online	7. customers
4. goal	

Part B Answers	
1. verb	4. verb
2. noun	5. verb
3. noun	6. noun

6 Applying Reading Skills (page 80)

Part A

1. Have the class look at the description of the reading skill. Make sure students understand what *organizing information in a chart* means.
2. Draw a three-column chart on the board with the heads *Who? What?* and *Why?* at the top of each column. Write *Cascadian Farms* under *Who?*
3. Start to fill in the chart with the help of the class. Using the list of verb phrases above the chart in the book, ask students a series of questions, such as *Do they make online games?* (*no*) *Do they play FarmVille?* (*no*), and so on. When students give the correct answer (*needs to advertise*), write it in the *What?* column in the chart on the board. Then ask students *Why do they need to advertise?* (*to tell people about their products*) and point out the filled-in answer in the *Why?* column in the chart in the book. Have students complete the chart in the book with a partner.

Answers

WHAT?

needs to advertise

makes online games

play FarmVille

work on a virtual farm

Part B

1. Have students work individually to complete the chart.
2. To check answers as a class, have students complete a blank chart on the board with *Who? What?* and *Why?* columns, as in the book.

Answers

WHAT?

FarmVille players: grow Cascadian Farms fruit

FarmVille players: buy real Cascadian Farms products / shop in real stores

The BMW, Apple, and Coca-Cola companies: pay money to movie makers

7 Discussion (page 80)

1. Start the discussion of question 1 by eliciting some common examples of computer games that you think your students may be familiar with (such as Solitaire) and write them on the board.
2. For question 2, make sure students give reasons for their answers.
3. For question 3, prompt students with examples, if necessary, from popular TV shows or recent movies.

Chapter 11 Guerilla Marketing

1 Topic Preview (page 81)

Part A

1. Have students look at the picture. Ask questions, such as *What do you see in the picture? What is the young man doing? What is he sitting on?*
2. Explain the meaning of *guerilla marketing*. (It comes from *guerilla warfare*, in which fighters use unusual or irregular types of warfare such as ambush. Therefore, in this case, it means a way of marketing that doesn't follow the rules.) Make sure students understand the task.
3. After students complete their answers, have a class discussion about why they do or do not pay attention to advertising.

Part B

1. For question 1, ask *What does the bench look like?* Ask students if they have ever seen a bench like this.
2. For question 2, ask *Why is there writing on the bench?* Elicit ideas about the purpose of the bench. Ask students if they are familiar with the product (KitKat candy).
3. For question 3, remind students of the meaning of *guerilla marketing*. Ask *What is surprising about the picture? What are some unusual or surprising ways to advertise products?*

2 Vocabulary Preview (page 82)

Part B Answers

1. unique	6. cheap
2. ad	7. equipment
3. artistic	8. message
4. sculpture	9. location
5. graffiti	10. imagination

3 Reading (pages 83–84)

This reading is about guerilla marketing, unconventional advertising that uses imagination to create unusual ads that get people's attention. It describes the characteristics of guerilla marketing and gives examples.

1. Introduce the reading with a class discussion about the pictures. Ask students to first describe each picture and then try to explain the purpose of the item or items they see in the pictures. Explain any new vocabulary that appears in the ads. Elicit or tell students that the first picture is an ad for a gym, the second is an ad for barbecue equipment, and the third is for a supermarket in the United Kingdom (ASDA). Ask students to give their opinion of each ad: *Do you like it? Why or why not?*
2. Before they start reading, have students preview the questions in Part A of the Reading Check on page 85.

4 Reading Check (page 85)

Part A Answers

1. F	2. T	3. T

Part B Answers

1. c	3. c	5. a	7. a
2. b	4. c	6. b	8. a

5 Vocabulary Check (page 86)

Part A Answers

1. ads	5. sculptures
2. locations	6. equipment
3. artistic	7. message
4. graffiti	8. imagination

Part B Answers

1. locations	4. imagination
2. cheap	5. unique
3. equipment	

6 Applying Reading Skills (page 87)

Part A

1. Look at the description of the reading skill with students and review the concept of asking "Why?" questions about a reading.
2. Point out that asking "Why?" questions about a reading is one of the most important critical thinking skills because it helps readers to better understand and remember important information.
3. Do the first "Why?" question with the class to make sure everyone understands how to do the activity. Then have students complete the task. When they finish, have them compare answers with a partner and then go over the answers with the class.

Possible Answers

Why did the note in the car say, "Feel free to get inside and move the car"?
A company wants you to try the car.

Why is guerilla marketing unique?
It's artistic and it's in everyday locations.

Why is guerilla marketing cheap?
It doesn't need a lot of expensive materials.

Part B

1. This task requires students to look back at the reading on pages 83–84. Clarify the instructions as needed.
2. Students can complete the activity in pairs, or if time is short, you can divide the class in half. Have one group work on item 1 and the other group work on item 2.

Possible Answers

Why is guerilla marketing artistic?
Why do companies love guerilla marketing?

7 Discussion (page 87)

1. For questions 1 and 2, make sure students give reasons for their answer.
2. For question 3, if time permits, put students into pairs or groups. Have them first discuss their answers to all of the questions and take notes. Then have them choose a group member to draw a picture of the ad. Have them choose another group member to present the ad to the class.

Chapter 12 The Land of Poyais

1 Topic Preview (page 88)

Part A

1. Make sure students understand the task. Give an example, if necessary, perhaps from your own background: *My grandfather moved to this county to get a better job.* Make sure students understand the vocabulary in each of the choices.
2. After students have checked their answers, go over their answers with the class.

Part B

1. For question 1, ask students to describe the picture. Have them try to guess where it is. Ask *Do you know any places like the one in the picture? What does it look like?*
2. For question 3, discuss the title of the reading. Pronounce *Poyais* for the class [po-YAY-is]. Ask them to guess what the connection is between the title and the picture.

2 Vocabulary Preview (page 89)

Part B Answers

1. traveler	6. trip
2. tourist	7. publicity
3. resources	8. promise
4. persuade	9. area
5. destination	10. campaign

3 Reading (pages 90–91)

This reading is about a real estate hoax that occurred in the nineteenth century. It gives the background of the man who perpetrated the hoax and explains how his marketing campaign convinced many people in Great Britain that not only was the place real, but that they should buy land there without even seeing it.

1. Introduce the reading with a class discussion about the pictures. Start with the map. Ask students to tell you what they know about this region. Ask questions, such as *What countries are in this part of the world? What are the countries like? What is the weather like there?* and so on. Have them look at the portrait of Gregor MacGregor and try to guess the time in which he lived and the kind of work he did. Then have students look at the currency and try to guess what it is and/or what it's for. Remind them of the title of the passage to help them answer these questions.
2. Have students predict whether this story is about the present or the past. Then have them try to answer this question: *Is Poyais a real place?*
3. Before they start reading, have students preview the questions in Part A of the Reading Check on page 92.

4 Reading Check (page 92)

Part A Answers

1. F	2. T	3. F

Part B Answers

1. b	3. b	5. b	7. b
2. c	4. c	6. b	

5 Vocabulary Check (page 93)

Part A Answers

1. campaign	6. travelers
2. promises	7. tourists
3. resources	8. trip
4. publicity	9. destination
5. persuaded	10. area

Part B Answers

1. b	3. b	5. a
2. a	4. a	

6 Applying Reading Skills (page 94)

Part A

1. Have the class look at the description of the reading skill. Make sure students understand what *order of events* means.
2. Draw a numbered list on the board. Read the list of events in Part A and make sure students understand them. Then ask *What happened first?* Elicit and write *MacGregor became a pirate* next to number 1 on the board. Then ask students *What happened after that?* and so on. Make sure they find the answers in the list on page 94.
3. Have students complete the list in the book with a partner.

Answers

1. MacGregor became a pirate.
2. MacGregor went to the coast of Central America.
3. MacGregor met a chief and got some land.
4. MacGregor got an idea: Invent Poyais and sell Poyais land.
5. MacGregor went back to Great Britain and advertised Poyais.

Part B

1. Have students work individually to number the steps in the correct order.
2. Check answers as a class by having volunteers write the steps in order on the board.

Answers

1 (e) There was a lot of publicity about Poyais.
2 (b) Many people believed the publicity.
3 (f) Many people bought Poyais land.
4 (d) More than 200 people sailed to Poyais.
5 (c) The people got to Poyais and learned the truth.
6 (a) Some people went home, and others stayed in Central America.

7 Discussion (page 94)

1. For question 1, have students give examples of ads they think do not tell the truth. If possible, bring print ads to class that may or may not be honest, and discuss them with your students. Ask them how they know whether an ad is honest.
2. For question 3, time permitting, put students into small groups to create the ad. Have them vote on a place to advertise and talk about the best way to advertise it. Then have them choose a student to draw a picture of the ad and another student to present the ad to the class. Have the class ask questions about each group's ad and/or vote on the best or most persuasive ad.

Unit 4 Wrap-Up

Vocabulary Review (page 95)

Answers

1. online	7. cheap
2. customer	8. imagination
3. advertise	9. tourist
4. awareness	10. promise
5. graffiti	11. destination
6. location	12. resources

Vocabulary in Use (page 96)

Answers will vary

Interview (page 96)

1. Introduce the activity by asking the class to think about all three stories. Have students review the titles and the pictures for each of the three chapters.
2. Explain that the students are going to ask each other the questions. Check that they understand the questions. Then put them into pairs. Have students take turns asking and answering the questions. Tell them to listen for differences in their answers and to discuss those differences.

Writing (page 96)

1. Explain the task and any unfamiliar vocabulary in the sentences in the list. Have students work in pairs to number the sentences. Go over the order of the sentences with the class.
2. Write the first two sentences of the paragraph on the board in paragraph form. Have students copy them and then complete the paragraph using the numbered list.
3. Have a volunteer write the complete paragraph on the board. Have students compare their paragraph with the one on the board.

Answers

1 (d) FarmVille is an online game.
2 (c) The players work on a farm and earn virtual money.
3 (b) The players can grow Cascadian Farms fruit on the farm.
4 (a) They learn all about the Cascadian Farms brand.
5 (f) Then the players become Cascadian Farms customers in real stores.
6 (e) Cascadian Farms is happy because their sales are going up.

FarmVille is an online game. The players work on a farm and earn virtual money. The players can grow Cascadian Farms fruit on the farm. They learn all about the Cascadian Farms brand. Then the players become Cascadian Farms customers in real stores. Cascadian Farms is happy because their sales are going up.

WebQuest (page 96)

At the time of publication, the links in the WebQuests were accurate and the content was deemed to be appropriate. However, Web sites change over time. It is therefore recommended that you go to the Web sites before assigning the WebQuests to make sure that the links are still current and the content is relevant and appropriate for your students. We continually monitor the Web sites and will make changes to the questions if the Web sites change or disappear. In such cases, you will have to work out the answers to those questions yourself.

Answers

1. two
2. sheep / horse / duck / rabbit
3. CityVille / Pioneer Trail
4. paper towels
5. coffee cup / popsicle / ice cream
6. New York / Los Angeles
7. 24 December 1786 / December 24, 1786
8. green and white
9. David Sinclair
10. a. *Mission: Impossible* / *Independence Day*
    b. *Cast Away*
    c. *Back to the Future*

5 TV and Film Studies

For general suggestions on how to teach each section of a unit, see pages v–vii of this Teacher's Manual.

Unit Opener (page 97)

1. With books closed, write *TV and Film Studies* on the board. Activate students' background knowledge with a class brainstorm. Ask students for words that are related to TV and film (*actor*, *actress*, *movie*, *show*, *program*, *Hollywood*).
2. Ask students questions, such as *Do you watch television? Which television shows do you enjoy? Which television shows do you not like? Do you like movies? Which movies do you like? Which movies do you not like? Did you watch movies as a child? Which actors/actresses do you like? Which movies were they in?*
3. Have students look at the content areas at the bottom of the page. Explain that each chapter will be about TV and film, but it will also relate to one of these content areas: sociology, psychology, and language studies. (*Sociology is the study of society and groups of people in society. Psychology is the study of the human mind and feelings.* To talk about language studies, say *We study English in this class. Do you study other languages?*)
4. Look at the titles of the three chapters and the short "teaser" blurbs about the readings. Make sure students understand these blurbs, especially the words *mean* and *uncomfortable*.

Chapter 13 Mean Judges

1 Topic Preview (page 98)

Part A

1. Have students describe the picture to a partner and then share their ideas with the class. Use the picture to teach the words *judge* and *contest*. Ask *Who are the four people? What do they do?*
2. Introduce Part A. Make sure students know they can check more than one item.
3. Have students share their answers in small groups. Then ask *Did anyone win a contest? How did it feel to win?*

Part B

1. Have students read the chapter title and look at the picture. Ask students what they think the word *mean* means.
2. For question 1, ask *How does the loser of a contest feel? How do you know? What does he or she do? How does he or she look?*
3. For question 2, ask students to describe the judges. Provide prompts if necessary. *Does he look unhappy? Does he look angry? Does she look nice? Is he handsome? Is she smiling?*
4. Have students revisit the title and make predictions about the story they are about to read.

2 Vocabulary Preview (page 99)

Part B Answers

1. tune in	6. contestant
2. expert	7. TV viewer
3. popular	8. status
4. reality TV	9. style
5. audience	10. behavior

3 Reading (pages 100–101)

This reading is about mean judges in reality show competitions on TV. Both audiences and contestants like mean judges. Contestants trust the opinions of a mean judge. TV audiences enjoy the mean judge because he or she makes them feel superior to the contestants. There are mean judges in countries throughout the world.

1. Introduce the reading with a discussion about the picture. Start with the picture of the happy contestant on page 100. Ask questions, such as *Where is this person? What is she doing? Why is she so happy?* Then have students look at the picture on page 101. *Where is this person? What is he doing? What do you think is the connection between the pictures and the title?*
2. Before they start reading, have students preview the questions in Part A of the Reading Check on page 102.

4 Reading Check (page 102)

Part A Answers

1. T	2. F	3. T

Part B Answers

1. c	3. b	5. c	7. b
2. b	4. a	6. a	

5 Vocabulary Check (page 103)

Part A Answers

1. reality TV	6. audience
2. tune in	7. behavior
3. contestant	8. TV viewers
4. popular	9. status
5. expert	10. style

Part B Answers

1. contestant	4. popular
2. audience	5. reality
3. viewer	

6 Applying Reading Skills (page 104)

Part A

1. Have the class look at the description of the reading skill and make sure they understand the concepts of *main ideas* and *supporting details*.
2. Explain that each paragraph has one main idea. Have students read paragraph 4. Ask *Who is the paragraph about?* Write the first sentence on the board: *Simon Cowell is a famous mean judge on reality TV.* Say *This is the main idea. Tell me something else about Simon Cowell.* (*He is nasty. He doesn't like most of the contestants.*) *These are supporting details about Simon.*
3. Have students complete the task with a partner. Review the answers with the class to make sure students understand the difference between main ideas and details.

Answers

Main idea 1: Supporting details are *a* and *d*.

Main idea 2: Supporting details are *b* and *c*.

Part B

1. Have students read paragraph 7 (the last paragraph) again.
2. Have students find supporting details on their own and then compare answers with a partner. Then check answers as a class.

Possible Answers

a. Millions of people tune in and watch these unpleasant judges.

b. The contestants try to please these judges.

7 Discussion (page 104)

1. For questions 1 and 2, have students describe reality shows in their countries. Have them describe the judges.
2. Have students discuss question 3 in small groups or pairs. Then take a poll about the anwers. Have students share their reasons with the whole class.

Chapter 14 The Uncanny Valley

1 Topic Preview (page 105)

Part A

1. Have students briefly describe the pictures to a partner. Ask *Who is she? What does she do?* Use the pictures to teach the word *robot*.
2. Review the directions with the class and be sure that students understand the task. Explain that they can check more than one answer.
3. Once students complete the task, ask *Are there are other differences between robots and humans?*

Part B

1. Before students discuss the questions, have them read the chapter title and look at the pictures again. Explain *uncanny* and *valley*. Tell students *You will learn about the uncanny valley in this reading.*
2. For question 2, ask students if the feeling is a good feeling or bad feeling. Encourage them to explain why they feel that way. They can refer back to the differences in Part A to help them.

2 Vocabulary Preview (page 106)

Part B Answers

1. emotion	6. anxious
2. scare	7. filmmaker
3. technology	8. computer-generated
4. animated	9. cartoon
5. response	10. positive

3 Reading (pages 107–108)

This reading is about how humans react to computer-generated movie characters. A Japanese scientist learned that we like robots more when they look more human, but at one point, when they look too human, our reactions suddenly change. This sudden change is called the "uncanny valley." The same situation is true with computer-generated movie characters. Filmmakers try to avoid the uncanny valley by creating cartoonlike characters rather than really humanlike characters.

1. Introduce the reading with a discussion about the pictures. First, have students look at Mori's graph on page 107. Give them time to study it. Point to the horizontal line and ask *What does this line show?* Then point to the vertical arrow and ask *What does this line show?* (*The horizontal line shows how humanlike something is. The vertical arrow shows how much we like that.*) Ask *Which part is the uncanny valley?*
2. Have students look at the picture of Wall-E on page 108. Ask *How do you feel about this little robot? Does he look like a human?*
3. Before they start reading, have students preview the questions in Part A of the Reading Check on page 109.

4 Reading Check (page 109)

Part A Answers

1. a 2. c 3. b

Part B Answers

1. T	4. T	7. T	10. F
2. F	5. T	8. T	
3. T	6. F	9. T	

5 Vocabulary Check (page 110)

Part A Answers

1. animated	6. cartoons
2. anxious	7. positive
3. emotions	8. technology
4. filmmakers	9. scare
5. computer-generated	10. response

Part B Answers

1. uncomfortable	3. good
2. feelings	4. frighten

6 Applying Reading Skills (page 111)

Part A

1. Look at the description of the reading skill. Explain the relationship between cause and effect. Write two sentences on the board. Ask students to identify which is the cause and which is the effect, for example, *He told a funny story.* (*cause*) *His friend laughed.* (*effect*)
2. Have students draw arrows from the causes to the effects in the chart.

Answers

1. b 2. c 3. a

Part B

1. This task requires students to look back at the reading on pages 107–108 to complete the chart. Do the first one together as a class.
2. Have students complete the chart on their own and then compare their answers with a partner.

Possible Answers

1. Suddenly our feelings change. / We don't like these human-looking robots at all!
2. CG humans seem dead.
3. Animators made a new Princess Fiona.

7 Discussion (page 111)

1. For questions 1 and 2, students will reflect on their own experience. After they have answered the questions in their groups, choose two or three examples of favorite characters. Draw a copy of Mori's graph on the board. Ask students where to place these characters.
2. For question 3, have students share their group's ideas with the class.

Chapter 15
A New Language

1 Topic Preview (page 112)

Part A

1. Have students describe the picture to a partner. The characters in the picture may be familiar to some. It may be helpful at this point to put students in pairs so that those who have seen the movie *Avatar* are paired with partners who haven't.
2. Ask *What new languages do you want to learn? Why? Did you ever teach your language to someone?* Make sure students understand the task and that they may check more than one answer. Have students complete the task and share answers with a partner.
3. Take a poll about the skills that are most difficult in a new language.

Part B

1. Before students discuss the questions, have them read the chapter title and look at the picture again.
2. For question 1, ask *Do you watch movies in English? Do you watch movies in other languages?*
3. For question 2, follow up by asking about other science fiction movies. Ask *Do aliens usually speak real languages in movies?*
4. For question 3, have students revisit the title and make predictions about the story they are about to read.

2 Vocabulary Preview (page 113)

Part B Answers

1. grammar	6. translate
2. set	7. vowel
3. create	8. consonant
4. project	9. director
5. (film) crew	10. pronunciation

3 Reading (pages 114–115)

This reading is about a new language, Na'vi, that was created for the movie Avatar. *Paul Frommer, a linguist, created the language based on some words invented by the movie director, James Cameron. The language has many fans and is a growing language.*

1. Introduce the reading with a class discussion about the pictures. First, have students look at the picture on page 114. *Where is the man on the left? What kind of work does he do?* Second, have students look at the picture on page 115. *What do you think the strange words are? Who is this man? What do you think is the connection between the two men? How are they related to the aliens in the picture on page 112?*
2. Before they start reading, have students preview the questions in Part A of the Reading Check on page 116.

4 Reading Check (page 116)

Part A Answers

1. b	2. a	3. c

Part B Answers

1. a	3. c	5. c	7. a
2. a	4. b	6. c	

5 Vocabulary Check (page 117)

Part A Answers

1. director	6. set
2. project	7. crew
3. consonants	8. translated
4. vowels	9. pronunciation
5. grammar	10. create

Part B Answers

1. project	4. English
2. movie set	5. word order
3. translate	

6 Applying Reading Skills (page 118)

Part A

1. Look at the description of the reading skill with students. Explain that they can learn to read faster. Point out that reading quickly is important in classes. Reading faster will also make reading easier and more fun.
2. Make sure students understand how to time themselves and how to calculate words per minute. Tell them there is no "correct" amount of time in which to complete a reading. Rather, they should work on improving their reading speed over time and with a lot of practice. Encourage students to read without using a dictionary.
3. Students who have their own stopwatches on their cell phones can time themselves.
4. Help students calculate their reading speed.

Part B

1. In this part, students will time themselves as they reread a different text. Students can choose either "Mean Judges" on pages 100–101 or "The Uncanny Valley" on pages 107–108.
2. Have students calculate their reading speeds. Ask *Which story was easier? Which story did you read faster?* They probably read the easier article faster.
3. Have a class discussion about how to read faster. Ask students for ideas. Provide ideas as well, for example: *Try not to use your dictionary. Ignore words you don't know. Use your finger to follow the words. Read in chunks. Look for main ideas.*
4. Encourage students to practice timing themselves outside of class.

7 Discussion (page 118)

1. For question 1, have students think about movies in their own language that feature alien characters. Ask *What kind of language do they speak? Does it sound like a real language?*
2. For question 2, start the discussion by asking if students know of any other man-made languages. (Klingon from *Star Trek* is probably the most famous language from movies. Esperanto is an example of one not associated with movies.) Ask *Would you like to learn Na'vi? Does it seem difficult or easy?*
3. In question 3, students are creating original words similar to what Paul Frommer did. After they have created three words, have them share their favorite word in small groups. Discuss why it was hard or easy to create these words. Ask *Would you enjoy creating a new language?*

Unit 5 Wrap-Up

Vocabulary Review (page 119)

Answers

1. expert	7. anxious
2. audience	8. cartoon
3. behavior	9. set
4. tune in	10. create
5. positive	11. translate
6. scare	12. project

Vocabulary in Use (page 120)

Answers will vary

Interview (page 120)

1. Introduce the activity by asking the class to think about all three stories. Have students review the titles and the pictures for each of the three chapters.
2. Explain that the students are going to ask each other the questions. Check that they understand the questions. Then put them into pairs. Have students take turns asking and answering the questions. Tell them to listen for differences in their answers and to discuss those differences.

Writing (page 120)

1. Review the main points about the three characters listed. Ask *Who is this person? What story was he in?*
2. Have students choose their favorite person from the list. Put students in small groups according to their favorite person. Have them discuss these questions: *What is his job? What did he do?*
3. Then have students work individually to write a paragraph about their favorite person.

WebQuest (page 120)

At the time of publication, the links in the WebQuests were accurate and the content was deemed to be appropriate. However, Web sites change over time. It is therefore recommended that you go to the Web sites before assigning the WebQuests to make sure that the links are still current and the content is relevant and appropriate for your students. We continually monitor the Web sites and will make changes to the questions if the Web sites change or disappear. In such cases, you will have to work out the answers to those questions yourself.

Answers

1. 2002
2. "Hell's Kitchen" / "Kitchen Nightmares" / "MasterChef"
3. "You're fired."
4. Masahiro Mori
5. Cubo girl
6. *The Incredibles*
7. 2009
8. `eylan
9. two
10. Answers will vary.

Unit Tests

Name: ______________________

Date: ______________________

PART ONE: **Reading Comprehension**
Read the story. Then answer the questions on pages 34–35.

Learning a Thousand Words

How do people learn information? How do people remember new words? John Pilley wants to know the answers. Professor Pilley studies learning. He has a helper named Chaser. Chaser is very smart. She has an excellent memory. She can learn many words. Who is Chaser? She is Professor Pilley's dog!

How many words can Chaser learn? Professor Pilley wants to know. He is doing an experiment. It works like this: Professor Pilley gives names to all of Chaser's toys. For example, he calls one toy "Emma." He says the names many times. Chaser likes the game. She is alert. She focuses on the professor. She listens to each name and looks at each toy. Then Professor Pilley puts the toys together. He says, "Find Emma." What is the result? Chaser finds the right toy! This shows something important about Chaser's brain. Chaser can match words to objects. Babies learn to match words to objects, too.

How does Chaser remember new words? She learns by hearing the names of her toys many times. Babies learn words in a similar way. But the dog often needs to hear a name 40 times. Professor Pilley interacts with Chaser for 4 or 5 hours a day. He says the words again and again.

Chaser can do something else. She can learn new words by herself. Professor Pilley puts a new toy with the old toys. He gives the new toy a name – Bob. But he doesn't teach this name to Chaser. He also doesn't show Chaser the new toy. Then he says "Get Bob." Chaser looks at all the toys. She chooses the new toy. It's Bob!

Some dogs can understand about 165 words. Chaser knows more than 1,000 words! Professor Pilley is a very good teacher. But Chaser is an excellent student!

Name: ______________________________

A Are these sentences *T* (true) or *F* (false)? (2 points each)

1. _____ Professor Pilley is an English teacher.
2. _____ Professor Pilley's helper is his dog.
3. _____ Professor Pilley is teaching Chaser to speak.
4. _____ Chaser knows less than 1,000 words.

B Circle the letter of the best answer. (2 points each)

1. What is Chaser helping Professor Pilley study?
   a. how people learn b. how people hear c. how people play with toys
2. What does Professor Pilley *not* use in his experiment?
   a. many dogs b. many words c. many toys
3. Why does Chaser listen to Professor Pilley?
   a. because she likes new toys
   b. because she knows him well
   c. because she likes the game
4. What does Professor Pilley learn from the experiment with Bob?
   a. Chaser needs to hear every new name again and again.
   b. Chaser can only learn the names of old toys.
   c. Chaser can learn new names by herself.
5. What sentence best describes Chaser?
   a. She is a good teacher.
   b. She is not a good dog.
   c. She is a good learner.

C Write short answers to these questions. (3 points each)

1. How many words can some other dogs learn?

   ____
2. How many words does Chaser know?

   ____
3. Who can usually learn new words more quickly – a baby or Chaser?

   ____
4. How many hours each day does Professor Pilley work with Chaser?

   ____

Name: ______________________________

PART TWO: Vocabulary

A The words in the box are from the main content area of the unit. Choose the best word to complete each sentence. You will not use all the words. (2 points each)

absent	budget	curriculum	drop out
graduate (*n.*)	information	score (*n.*)	study (*v.*)

1. That book is very good. There is a lot of very useful ______________________ in it.
2. My brother is a ______________________ of New York University.
3. Everyone is here today. No one is ______________________.
4. We like all our classes. Our school has a great ______________________.
5. There is not enough money in the school ______________________. We cannot buy more books.

B Circle the letter of the best word to complete each sentence. The answer is always an Academic Word List word from the unit. (2 points each)

1. Many students learn better when they play games and _______ with others.

   a. focus   b. interact   c. govern   d. vote

2. When the TV is too loud, I can't _______ on my reading.

   a. focus   b. relax   c. drop out   d. study

3. In some countries, a young person becomes a / an _______ at age 21.

   a. result   b. rule   c. score   d. adult

4. _______ can cause many health problems.

   a. Administration   b. Curriculum   c. Stress   d. Information

5. Writing is a good way to _______ before a test or a big game.

   a. relax   b. study   c. drop out   d. interact

Test • Unit 2

Name: ____________________

Date: ____________________

PART ONE: Reading Comprehension
Read the story. Then answer the questions on pages 38–39.

Teenage Shoppers

At a shopping mall, two teenage girls see a store with an odd design. It looks like a beach house. Do they go in? Yes! The store smells nice. There is good music, and it's loud. There is a video of surfers on a big TV. There are cool[1] things on the wall to look at. The clothes are bright and colorful and soft to touch. This is fun! The girls are happy in the store. They don't want to leave. The store's design is a success.

Clothing stores compete with other clothing stores. They want teenagers to come into their store. They want teenagers to stay in their store. But why do stores want teenagers? Why not parents or seniors? The answer is simple. Teenagers have money, and they like to spend it. Here are some facts about teenagers:

- There are over 30 million teenagers in the United States. This is the largest teenage population since 1960.
- Many teenagers have jobs. They have money to spend.
- Teenagers often receive gift cards for special events like birthdays. Many of them (78 percent) use these gift cards instead of money to shop.
- Teenagers stay at the mall for a long time. How long is each visit? Most teenagers (68 percent) spend more than 2 hours there.
- Female teenagers spend more money on clothes than male teenagers.

Back at the clothing store, a teenage boy assists the girls. He's wearing cool clothes from the store. He looks about their age. The girls think, "We have something in common with him." This isn't just *a* store, it's *their* store. The girls stay a long time. And they spend a lot of money!

---

[1] *cool:* fashionable and interesting

Name: ______________________________

A Are these sentences *T* (true) or *F* (false)? (2 points each)

1. _____ The design of a store is important to teenage shoppers.
2. _____ Stores want teenagers to leave quickly.
3. _____ Some stores want teenage customers more than older customers.
4. _____ Teenagers usually stay at the mall for about an hour.

B Circle the letter of the best answer. (2 points each)

1. What helps stores get teenage customers?

   a. seniors work in the stores b. nice smells c. beaches

2. Why do teenagers stay in some clothing stores?

   a. They watch fun videos.
   b. They like the dark colors.
   c. They hear quiet music.

3. About how many teenagers are in the United States?

   a. 10 million b. 30 million c. 50 million

4. Which sentences describes teenage shoppers?

   a. Most teenage shoppers prefer to use gift cards.
   b. Most teenage shoppers prefer to use money.
   c. Most teenage shoppers like both equally.

5. What percent of teenagers stay at the mall for over 2 hours?

   a. 68 percent b. 78 percent c. 90 percent

C Write short answers to these questions. (3 points each)

1. What does the store look like?

   ____

2. What are two things the girls like about the store?

   ____

3. Why do stores want teenagers?

   ____

4. Who spends more money on clothes, girls or boys?

   ____

 Name: ______________________________

PART TWO: Vocabulary

A The words in the box are from the main content area of the unit. Choose the best word to complete each sentence. You will not use all the words. (2 points each)

elderly	in charge	independent	movement
reaction	reality	relatives	respect (*n.*)

1. The pictures of the hotel on the Web site are very nice. But in ______________________, it is not a nice place at all.
2. He is planning a trip to China to visit his ______________________.
3. She is the administrator of the school. She is ______________________ of the teachers, the students, and the school building.
4. His father is 80, but he wants to live alone. He wants to be ______________________.
5. In many offices, there is a / an ______________________ to use less paper.

B Circle the letter of the best word to complete each sentence. The answer is always an Academic Word List word from the unit. (2 points each)

1. The first day of the Olympics is a busy day for the _______. The reporters and photographers want to interview the athletes and take their pictures.

   a. tribe b. royalty c. media d. characters

2. That building is a very _______ color. It's unusual to see a bright orange library!

   a. odd b. fictional c. elderly d. independent

3. The people's _______ to the new town park is very good. Everyone loves it!

   a. movement b. design c. reaction d. media

4. Families stay together in many cultures. _______, elderly parents live with their children.

   a. Differently b. Early c. Traditionally d. Completely

5. Many stores need extra workers to _______ people during busy times.

   a. react to b. assist c. compete with d. perform a ritual for

Test • Unit 3

Name:

Date:

PART ONE: **Reading Comprehension**

Read the story. Then answer the questions on pages 42–43.

What a Memory!

Most people can remember important things. Louise Owen can remember almost everything! Ask her about July 16, 1999. She can tell you everything about that day. She can recall her food, her clothes, and her phone calls. Ask her about a news event. She can tell you all about it. Her memories are very visual. In her mind, she sees everything again.

To Owen, this is normal. But her kind of memory is rare. Most people can't remember everything. Only about 25 people in the world have this ability.

Researchers are studying people like Louise Owen. How are they different? Two parts of their brains are larger than normal. Is this the cause of unusual memory? Or is it the result? It isn't clear.

Researchers know the answer to this question: Is this kind of memory a symptom of another condition? "No" is the answer. These people are all very healthy.

People with this kind of memory have a lot in common. They wash their hands a lot. They are always collecting[1] things. They also need to have everything in order. Actress Marilu Henner, for example, always keeps her shoes and clothes in perfect order. Of course, these people put all their memories in order, too. Finally, people with unusual memory have one more thing in common. Most of them are not married.

Some of these people do not like their special ability. Why? They remember all the unhappy periods in their lives. They can never forget sad feelings. That can make life very difficult. But most people enjoy their amazing memory. They remember all the happy times. They never forget their friends. And they always win memory games!

---

[1] *collecting:* finding things and keeping them because you are interested in them

 Name: ______________________________

A Are these sentences *T* (true) or *F* (false)? (2 points each)

1. _____ Louise Owen can't remember much about July 16, 1999.
2. _____ Owen's memory is normal.
3. _____ Owen sees pictures of past events in her mind.
4. _____ Everyone with this kind of memory is happy about it.

B Circle the letter of the best answer. (2 points each)

1. Why is Louise Owen's memory unusual?
   a. She can remember important things.
   b. She can memorize a lot of information quickly.
   c. She can remember almost everything.
2. Do people with this kind of memory have an illness?
   a. Yes. b. No. c. Researchers don't know.
3. What do researchers know about people with this kind of memory?
   a. Two of the people have large brains.
   b. Two parts of their brains are very large.
   c. Their brains are normal.
4. Which question do researchers have about people with amazing memory?
   a. Why are their brains larger than normal?
   b. Are their brains the same as other people's brains?
   c. Is amazing memory the symptom of another condition?
5. Which of these sentences is *not* true about people with this kind of memory?
   a. They have nothing in common.
   b. Their memories are very visual.
   c. They want to put everything in order.

C Write short answers to these questions. (3 points each)

1. Why is Louise Owens different from other people?

   ____

2. How many people have this kind of memory?

   ____

3. What is one problem for people with this kind of memory?

   ____

4. What do people with this kind of memory have in common? Give one example.

   ____

 Name: ____________________

PART TWO: Vocabulary

A The words in the box are from the main content area of the unit. Choose the best word to complete each sentence. You will not use all the words. (2 points each)

dig	humans	mind	minerals
oxygen	rare	surface	temperature

1. They are not in the mine. They are above ground. They are on the ____________________.
2. What are gold and silver? They are ____________________.
3. Not many people have this condition. It's very ____________________.
4. People need this to live. People need ____________________.
5. His body ____________________ is 101° F (38.3° C).

B Circle the letter of the best word to complete each sentence. The answer is always an Academic Word List word from the unit. (2 points each)

1. A music player is a small _______. We use it to listen to music.
   a. drill b. diagram c. device d. period
2. A lot of people are sick, but I am not. This illness doesn't _______ me.
   a. affect b. dig c. cure d. survive
3. Everyone is worried about the miners. Will they _______?
   a. dig b. affect c. recall d. survive
4. Everyone waits a long time. _______, they get the good news.
   a. Correctly b. Finally c. Mentally d. Normally
5. Five minutes is a short _______ of time.
   a. period b. condition c. device d. ability

Name: ______________________

Date: ______________________

PART ONE: **Reading Comprehension**
Read the story. Then answer the questions on pages 46–47.

The Best Job in the World

There was a beautiful island in Australia. It was a perfect place for tourists. But there was a problem. Almost nobody visited the area. Not many people knew about it.

Some people on the island had an idea. They started a marketing campaign called "The Best Job in the World." They used their imagination to write an ad for the job. They put the ad online:

> THE BEST JOB IN THE WORLD
>
> **Caretaker[1] for Hamilton Island**
>
> Help us! Keep Hamilton Island beautiful. Live and work on a beach! Swim every day! Meet nice people! Make a lot of money! Is this the right job for you? Tell us about yourself. Send us a video.

This was a real ad for a real job. But it was a marketing campaign, too. The goal was to get a lot of attention for Hamilton Island. It worked! Seven million people visited the Web site and read the online message. Thirty-four thousand people applied for the job. They made 60-second videos about themselves. They talked about their skills. They put the videos on the site. Other people watched the videos. Then they voted for the best person for the job.

A British man named Ben Southall got the most votes. And he got the best job in the world! Southall lived on Hamilton Island for six months. He wrote about it and took pictures. He put his stories and pictures on the Internet. This also increased awareness of Hamilton Island. Now many people come to see the island.

The ad didn't cost a lot of money. In fact, it was cheap! But it got a lot of publicity for Hamilton Island. There's a very good reason for the amazing results: The "best job in the world" had the best marketing campaign in the world.

1 A *caretaker* keeps a place clean and safe

 Name: ______________________________

A Are these sentences *T* (true) or *F* (false)? (2 points each)

1. _____ Few tourists knew about Hamilton Island.
2. _____ The marketing campaign was not for a real job.
3. _____ The job ad cost a lot of money.
4. _____ The campaign was successful.

B Circle the letter of the best answer. (2 points each)

1. Where is Hamilton Island?

   a. in Britain b. in Australia c. in the United States

2. People put the job ad _______.

   a. in a video b. on the island c. on the Internet

3. What did people do in the videos?

   a. talk about Hamilton Island
   b. talk about themselves
   c. talk about the Web site

4. What did Ben Southall do on the island?

   a. He watched videos about the island.
   b. He made videos about his skills.
   c. He wrote about the island and took pictures.

5. What was the result of Southall's stories about the island?

   a. Many people visit the island.
   b. Many people write about the island.
   c. Many people visit the island's Web site.

C Write short answers to these questions. (3 points each)

1. What job is "the best job in the world"?

   ____

2. How did people apply for the job?

   ____

3. How many people applied for the job?

   ____

4. How did Ben Southall get the job?

   ____

 Name: ______________________________

PART TWO: Vocabulary

A The words in the box are from the main content area of the unit. Choose the best word to complete each sentence. You will not use all the words. (2 points each)

ad	advertise	brand	campaign
cheap	customer	product	publicity

1. The ______________________ is buying fruit at the store.
2. Her favorite ______________________ is Cascadian Farms.
3. This new computer isn't ______________________. It's expensive.
4. The company used the Internet to ______________________ the job.
5. There was a lot of ______________________ in the newspaper about the island. Now many people go there.

B Circle the letter of the best word to complete each sentence. The answer is always an Academic Word List word from the unit. (2 points each)

1. The store is in a good _______. A lot of people can see it there.

   a. equipment b. brand c. location d. message

2. They found _______ such as water and gold on the island.

   a. imagination b. publicity c. equipment d. resources

3. Women are the _______ of this ad for health food.

   a. target b. destination c. awareness d. customers

4. The _______ of the ad was to get more attention for the town.

   a. product b. goal c. brand d. location

5. The ad was successful. It increased _______ of the place by 100 percent.

   a. graffiti b. message c. area d. awareness

Test • Unit 5

Name: ______________________________

Date: ______________________________

PART ONE: **Reading Comprehension**

Read the story. Then answer the questions on pages 50–51.

Rin Tin Tin

He was a popular movie star in the 1920s. Audiences all over the world loved him! They sent him 10,000 letters a week. There are many stars in Hollywood, but this star was different. Why? He was a dog! His name was Rin Tin Tin.

The story starts in 1918. Lee Duncan was a soldier in World War I. He found a hungry little puppy[1] in France. He called him Rin Tin Tin. He took the dog back home to Los Angeles after the war.

Duncan put Rin Tin Tin in a dog show. The dog jumped over a 12-foot fence (4 meters)! A friend of Duncan's made a movie about this special dog. Duncan was excited. He showed the movie to many filmmakers. At Warner Brothers movie company, the film crew needed a wolf.[2] Duncan said, "Rin Tin Tin can do that." He was right! So Warner Brothers hired the dog. Rin Tin Tin was a big success. He made 26 movies for Warner Brothers. Before Rin Tin Tin, Warner Brothers had money problems. But Rin Tin Tin's movies made a lot of money. They saved the company!

Rin Tin Tin had status in Hollywood. He had his own chair on the movie set. His name was on the back of the chair, just like all the stars. He also had a special cook, and he ate steak every day. The dog was even in the Los Angeles phone book.

Rin Tin Tin died in 1932. Then Duncan trained Rin Tin Tin's puppies. He called them all Rin Tin Tin. They also made movies and TV shows. In the 1950s, *The Adventures of Rin Tin Tin* was a popular TV show. TV viewers loved all the Rin Tin Tins.

Today, Rin Tin Tin X (number 10) has a Facebook page. His owners say, "There will always be a Rin Tin Tin."

---

1 *puppy:* a very young dog
2 *wolf:* a wild animal, like a dog

 Name: ____________________

A Are these sentences *T* (true) or *F* (false)? (2 points each)

1. _____ The first Rin Tin Tin was born in Hollywood.
2. _____ Rin Tin Tin's movies were very popular.
3. _____ Rin Tin Tin's puppies were in *The Adventures of Rin Tin Tin*.
4. _____ People only like the first Rin Tin Tin.

B Circle the letter of the best answer. (2 points each)

1. The first Rin Tin Tin was popular _______.

   a. all over the world. b. in France c. in the United States
2. What happened to the first movie with Rin Tin Tin?
   a. Lee Duncan showed the movie to filmmakers.
   b. Warner Brothers bought the movie.
   c. Lee Duncan's friend sold the movie.
3. Who hired Rin Tin Tin?
   a. Lee Duncan's friend
   b. the film crew
   c. Warner Brothers movie company
4. Why was Rin Tin Tin important to Warner Brothers?
   a. He looked like a wolf.
   b. He was popular on TV.
   c. His movies made a lot of money.
5. What did Lee Duncan do when Rin Tin Tin died?
   a. He was the star of a TV show.
   b. He trained Rin Tin Tin's puppies.
   c. He was the director of *The Adventures of Rin Tin Tin*.

C Write short answers to these questions. (3 points each)

1. Where did Lee Duncan find Rin Tin Tin?

   ____
2. How many movies did Rin Tin Tin make?

   ____
3. How was the first Rin Tin Tin like a human star? Give one example.

   ____
4. How is today's Rin Tin Tin like a human?

   ____

Name: ____

PART TWO: Vocabulary

A The words in the box are from the main content area of the unit. Choose the best word to complete each sentence. You will not use all the words. (2 points each)

audience	cartoons	contestant	director
crew	reality TV	tune in	TV viewers

1. The ______________________ works together on a movie. They are in charge of the lights, cameras, and sound.
2. Children always love ______________________. They like to laugh at the funny characters.
3. Millions of people ______________________ to watch the Olympic Games on TV.
4. Only one ______________________ can win a competition on TV.
5. Everyone in the ______________________ loved the movie.

B Circle the letter of the best word to complete each sentence. The answer is always an Academic Word List word from the unit. (2 points each)

1. The students did a / an _______ together for film class. They worked on it for many weeks.

   a. director b. project c. emotion d. grammar

2. The professor is a / an _______ on old movies. He watches them a lot.

   a. status b. expert c. style d. behavior

3. He knows a lot about _______, such as computers.

   a. cartoons b. response c. contestants d. technology

4. A professor has a lot of _______ at a college.

   a. status b. audience c. pronunciation d. project

5. Everyone liked the new film a lot. Their responses were very _______.

   a. computer-generated b. creative c. positive d. anxious

Answer Key

Unit 1

PART ONE: Reading Comprehension

A

1. F
2. T
3. F
4. F

B

1. a
2. a
3. c
4. c
5. c

C

1. about 165 words
2. more than 1,000 words
3. a baby
4. 4 or 5 hours

PART TWO: Vocabulary

A

1. information
2. graduate
3. absent
4. curriculum
5. budget

B

1. b
2. a
3. d
4. c
5. a

Unit 2

PART ONE: Reading Comprehension

A

1. T
2. F
3. T
4. F

B

1. b
2. a
3. b
4. a
5. a

C

1. a beach house
2. videos (of surfers) / cool things on the walls; (loud) music; nice smells; the (bright colors of the) clothes; touching the soft clothes / (help from) the teenage boy
3. Teens have money, and they like to spend it.
4. girls

PART TWO: Vocabulary

A

1. reality
2. relatives
3. in charge
4. independent
5. movement

B

1. c
2. a
3. c
4. c
5. b

Unit 3

PART ONE: Reading Comprehension

A

1. F
2. F
3. T
4. F

B

1. c
2. b
3. b
4. a
5. a

C

1. She can remember almost everything.
2. about 25 people
3. They remember all the unhappy periods in their lives. / They cannot forget sad feelings.
4. They wash their hands a lot. / They collect things. / They put (or keep) everything in order. / They are not married.

PART TWO: Vocabulary

A

1. surface
2. minerals
3. rare
4. oxygen
5. temperature

B

1. c
2. a
3. d
4. b
5. a

Unit 4

PART ONE: Reading Comprehension

A

1. T
2. F
3. F
4. T

B

1. b
2. c
3. b
4. c
5. a

C

1. caretaker for Hamilton Island
2. They made videos.
3. 34,000
4. He got the most votes.

PART TWO: Vocabulary

A

1. customer
2. brand
3. cheap
4. advertise
5. publicity

B

1. c
2. d
3. a
4. b
5. d

Unit 5

PART ONE: Reading Comprehension

A

1. F
2. T
3. T
4. F

B

1. a
2. a
3. c
4. c
5. b

C

1. France
2. 26
3. He had his own chair. / His name was on the back of the chair. / He had a special cook. / He ate steak every day. / His name was in the Los Angeles phone book. / His movies made a lot of money.
4. He has a Facebook page.

PART TWO: Vocabulary

A

1. film crew
2. cartoons
3. tune in
4. contestant
5. audience

B

1. b
2. b
3. d
4. a
5. c

Track Listing

Track	Page	Title
1		Introduction
2	4	Late Start
3	11	First Write . . . It Helps!
4	18	Student Government
5	28	A Strange Place to Live!
6	35	King Peggy
7	42	Quidditch: The World of Harry Potter Comes to Life
8	52	Rescue in Chile
9	59	Sleeping Beauty
10	66	Memory Palace
11	76	FarmVille
12	83	Guerilla Marketing
13	90	The Land of Poyais
14	100	Mean Judges
15	107	The Uncanny Valley
16	114	A New Language